MW00979976

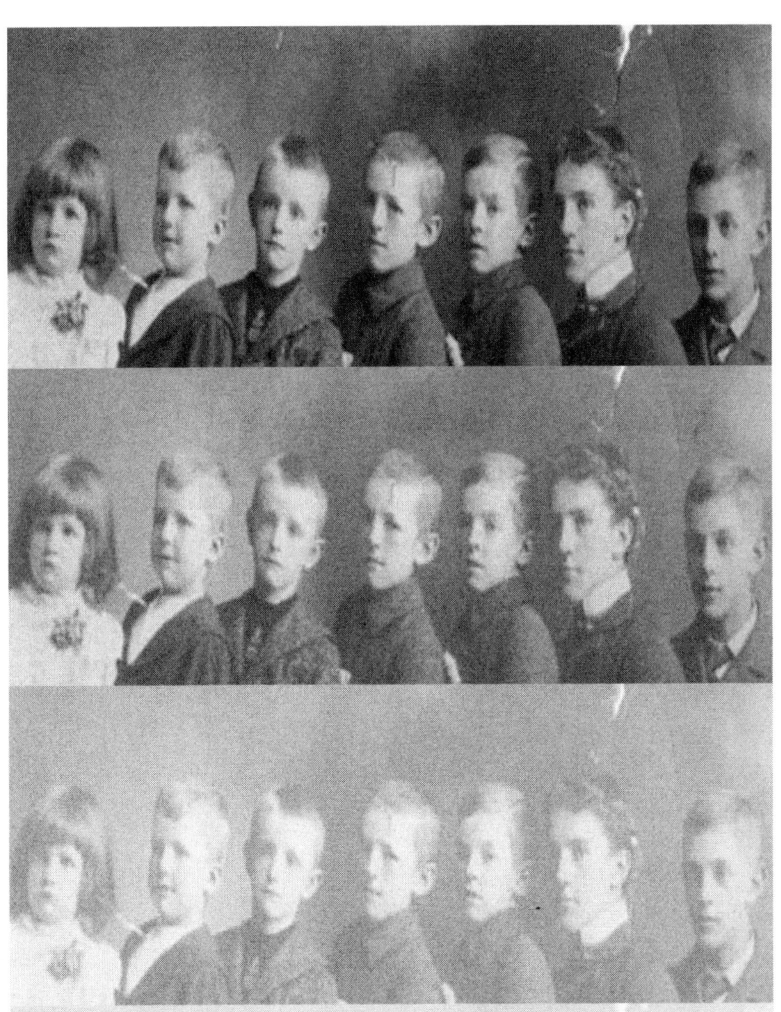

The Lost Boys

by R.H. Thomson

• IDENTITY – Diamond Grill
Fugitive Pieces (Ben)

• child of war survivor (Ben)

• mundane trivial concerns

→ being inside (w/ ancestors) family/history present at all times w/ the person now.

The Lost Boys

Letters From The Sons In Two Acts

1914 – 1923

by

R.H. Thomson

Playwrights Canada Press
Toronto • Canada

Playwrights Canada Press
54 Wolseley Street, 2nd Floor, Toronto, Ontario CANADA M5T 1A5
416-703-0013 fax 416-703-0059 info@puc.ca http://www.puc.ca

Playwrights Canada Press acknowledges the support of The Canada Council for the Arts for our publishing programme and the Ontario Arts Council.

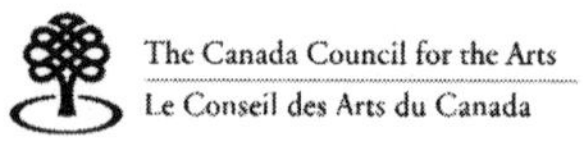

Photos:
Cover (*l to r*): Rick, Arthur, George, Joe, Jack, Harold and Graham Stratford.
page 7: *Le Reve* or *The Dream Of Soldiers* by Edouard Detaille. Catalogue No. AN19910216-056. Canadian War Museum.
page 17: German Soldiers (Q1229); page 40: The Road to Ypres (Q1163); page 51: Passchendaele – Before (57.v.82) After (21.B.316). Imperial War Museum.
Production Editor & Cover Design: Jodi Armstrong

National Library of Canada Cataloguing in Publication Data

Thomson, R.H.
The lost boys

A play.
ISBN 0-88754-634-X

1. World War, 1914-1918--Drama. 2. Thomson, R.H.--Family--Drama. I. Title.

PS8589.H5386L68 2002 C812'.6 C2001-904300-7
PR9199.4.H63L68 2002

First edition: January 2002.
Printed and bound by AGMV Marquis at Quebec, Canada.

To Miss Mayden Stratford,
my great aunt and the little sister to the Stratford boys.
Without Mayden's dedication to her brothers my journey
would never have happened.

I want to acknowledge those who helped guide me: Richard Rose, Eric Peterson, Stuart McLean, Jonas Jurasas, Micheline Chevrier.

I want also to acknowledge the Stratford family whose stories, permission and support enabled me to unearth so much personal history.

"There were a great number of young men who had never been in a war and were consequently far from unwilling to join in this one."
Thucydides, 5th century BCE

"If any question why we died,
Tell them because our fathers lied."
Rudyard Kipling, whose son was lost to the battlefields of World War I.

PLAYWRIGHT'S FOREWORD

The content of this play was assembled from the letters in my family, the regimental war diaries of the regiments in which my great uncles served, attestation papers, army medical records and histories of WWI. What surprised me in this personal search was not the wealth of detail available about that riddle called "The Great War," but rather those who came forward unasked and offered what they knew. Time and again, out of the blue I received letters, calls and e-mails from people who had heard of my search and wanted to contribute. At times it was uncanny. I am richer because of them.

The letters from my family span the years 1914 - 1923. Reading them is hearing only half of a conversation since I had only the letters which came west from Europe to Canada. All the letters travelling east were lost. The letters were from an array of family; brothers, mothers, aunts and cousins. They were also from strangers; ordinary soldiers, commanding officers, army bureaucrats and families who had billeted my great uncles in their homes.

While the play surrounds itself with the minutia of war, I never intended it to be about the war. The journeys which we undertake define us. I did not recognize the country which I was traversing until my feet were on the path. The landscape of our experience changes forever with our aging. What was possible in our youth is no longer possible now. Yet there are possibilities that exist in age which were never apparent in youth. I used to think that my great uncles, being dead, would have no meaning in my life. I now know that there is nothing without meaning.

My path led me to the indefinable places and it was frustrating to realize that the high meadows I sought were beyond the power of words. But on the way I gained more family than I ever realized I had. From the reactions of so many in the audience I now know that they were gaining their families as well.

—R.H. Thomson

The Lost Boys was first produced by The Great Canadian Theatre Company, Ottawa, March 15 to April 1, 2001 with the following cast and crew:

ACTOR (all roles)	R.H. Thomson

Recorded voices: Nancy Palk, Kate Hurman, Danielle Gregoire.

Directed by Jonas Jurasas
Set Design by Scott Windsor
Costume Design by Sue Fijalkowska
Lighting Design by Martin Conboy
Sound Design by Duncan Morgan
Stage Managed by Jennifer Strahl

Sound & Music Consultant	Don Horsburgh
Projections	Martin Conboy Barbara Cuerden
Image Manipulation	Danielle Dewar (MCLD)
Additional Photography	Elizabeth Feryn

CHARACTERS

MAN
CHAPUCHAPU
BOY
ART
THE ATTESTOR
JOE
GEORGE
MOTHER
JACK
OFFICER
MARGARET
MME MIALARET
RICK

ACT ONE

ACTOR wanders in mind and darkness with a WWI cavalry sword. He uses the sword to try to unearth a half-remembered vigil from his youth. The stage is a series of scrimmed screens on which appear the faces and war landscape of the play. The dreamscape.

MAN Swords thrilled me as a boy. They seemed always to be part of a great story; King Arthur and his Excalibur. Only the worthy got to hold the sword. The sword of "Justice." The sword of "Truth." The sword that separates the living from the dead, separates the foolish from the wise, illusion from reality. But this? This is an old cavalry sword that hung in my grandmother's house. The stuff of a six-year-old's fantasy... the cavalry, brilliant uniforms, dashing charges.

Only once in my life did I hold a sword for real. I'm embarrassed to remember it. It was the dead of night, I was only half awake. How did it go? I've buried this memory. It was a vigil. I was 16. That was a long time ago. To show that I was worthy of receiving the sword I had to say "I am here to..."

I was 16 and I was in Belgium. It was the usual European tour for teenagers... castles, Cathedrals etc. except for this all-night vigil. It was for the dead of the First World War. My vigil was in the actual battle chapel, a chapel created by the soldiers in the attic of a house in Belgium just behind the front line – which meant where all the fighting took place.

ACTOR enters the space, seats sword, and begins to light scattered candles.

For twenty minutes in the middle of the night I knelt alone. That time was "my watch" but what was I watching for? Leaning along that wall were short wooden crosses, I remember their crudeness. They were the original crosses from the battle-graves, temporary graves, dug in haste, assembled in the millions, before the military grave stones were cut and the dead were gathered into the official cemeteries... 2500 cemeteries... nine and a half million dead.

But the reality of the First War was dim. I mumbled my words, knelt for my vigil, gave back the sword and then stumbled back outside to the Belgian darkness. Standing there in the light of the stars I didn't get it, and of all the teenagers there, I should have been the one who did. Two of my great uncles were buried there. A number of my family had been killed by that war. Did I have any idea of the story surrounding me?

The ACTOR approaches the trunk containing the letters. The image of the brothers appears.

You see I have this family, and all these letters. The letters were a bit of a deal in my family. They were from five brothers, my great uncles, who had gone to fight in the First World War. The letters had been typed out and distributed. At 16 I'd read a few. There were hundreds of them. The adults kept saying how important they were. I never got very far... five brothers... I kept getting their names mixed up... and the repetition. "Could you send a couple of pairs of socks?" "Could you send moth balls?" "The Belgium mud is something fierce." "I could do with another pair of socks."

The trunk is opened. The five folders of letters emerge.

Five Stratford brothers went to war Art, Joe, George, Jack and Harold; five went to war and four never survived the experience. The letters were nearly all to their Mother, my great grandmother. Here's a letter that passed me by when I was 16. It's written from Military hospital, which was called "the butcher's shop" by some.

l to r: Rick, Art, George, Joe, Jack, Harold, Graham.

Only the initial letters are read, the rest are performed.

MAN "...I'm not brave, I've found that out since coming to France, but I think I can safely say that the couple of times I've been up against it I've stuck it out. I've seen things I haven't written home about Moth ["Moth" is mother] and which I'm trying my best to forget as soon as I can.

"There is a lad at the Hospital who has got a bullet three inches in his brain and it doesn't worry him a bit, he can talk, walk, etc. but the docs are awfully afraid it will shift and if it does it will be good-bye for him. Talking of my bullet, [this letter is from Art] I'll have to keep it for the rest of my life. I feel perfectly sure that I'm not going to get popped off. It's a funny feeling I have. I'm going to get wounded again, I am perfectly sure I am and it makes me very chirpy. Some fellows feel differently about it, that is they feel they are going to get plugged and they usually do. Now Moth don't worry about your boys. We'll all come back all right."

No, I didn't read this when I was 16. I feel now that these boys, these letters, the family have been waiting for me since I've been young, very young... just too many "markers" in my path... like the breadcrumbs dropped by Hansel and Gretel in the woods. The path led somewhere but I never followed.

The first of the "detonator" markers of the evening follow this point.

MAN/BOY There was a big picture. I was very small. It hung in the hall on the way to my grandmother's dining room. It was on the opposite wall to the dinner gong. I loved the dinner gong. I remember this picture for as far back as I can remember – six years old, three. The picture fascinated me. It was about dreams and the dawn. It was called "Le Reve."

The Dream Of Soldiers by Edouard Detaille

"The Dream Of Soldiers" is projected.

It's just before dawn, and in the sky above are the dreams of the soldiers who sleep. The dawn is very close. I was never sure how happy those dreams were, though the dream soldiers were marching proudly in the clouds. The real soldiers sleep on the ground, wrapped in their coats. The real soldiers are like my toys at my grandmother's house. Hundreds of guns are piled in the field. There are sounds coming from the picture, shouts and cries, but everything is somehow far away. I wonder about the other place above in the clouds. It's as if the dream soldiers were going to march off into the stars. And as I got older, a teenager maybe, it got clearer. It was about battle and death, and glory and victory.

The actor walks into the picture.

MAN And now that I am even older, I know it is about eternity, an eternity which is very close. I know now the dream soldiers marching in the clouds are dead, which is why their cries always came from somewhere far away. I know now that this picture hung in the house of a woman who had lost four brothers because of the war. That woman was my grandmother. Her brothers were my great uncles. Now that I think back on it, I know there were some mighty goings on in that house though I never realized it then. Why?

Art, Joe, George, Jack, Harold. They were all from Brantford, Ontario. I knew only one of the five brothers, the youngest, Art. Uncle Art as we all called him.

He was my mysterious and favourite uncle, my great uncle really. I know now that Art had a fantastical war; Belgium, Egypt, Royal Flying Corps, Africa.

Arthur Stratford

Art ended the war fighting with the King's African Rifles in what is now Mozambique. He spent a year and a half in Nyasaland chasing Germans on foot, but rarely actually seeing them. He spoke Chenyanja, Arabic. He wrote home about crocodiles "who don't go in for crowds." Here Art is in Africa being offered a wife. "...as I was walking down the road with one of my corporals I was practicing my vocabulary;
Kodi uli ndi wamkazzi pa linu?
[Have you a wife in camp?]
Ndio Bwana.
[Yes Sir.]

His corporal was Chapuchapu from the Angoni tribe. Chapuchapu was nicknamed Whiskers Barton.

Uli ndi akazi angati?
[How many wives have you?]
Awui Bwana pa Dedeeza ndipo, Madeezi apa.
[Three.]
Chabwino, uli moontu wa mwai!
[Good, you are a lucky man!]
Iai Bwana, chifiikwa chaini ufima modzi?
[Not at all lucky, would you like one?]

> *CHAPUCHAPU's image disappears. We return to the present.*

Art didn't accept but he did marry years later and it was tragic. What I remember most about Art, is the sound of his teeth, that clicking of early dentures. He called them his "china-clippers." Art told us of the "Allemand bullet" still buried beside his spine, "a hole the size of an 1/8 inch drill." He told of the Hun sniper hidden in the trees that rainy night in 1915. At the top of the stairs in my Grandmother's house lay more of Art's mysteries; ceremonial knife, Ngoni shield, club, knobkerri, drums. When he returned to Toronto in 1919, unannounced after 5 years of war, he slipped into the men's washroom at Union Station and removed his army uniform. He then proceeded to paint his ribs and face, and don feathered Zulu garb. Armed with the Ngoni shield and clutching the club and a few stabbing assegaisi, he then took the trolley through the Toronto streets to my grandmother's house. Again unannounced, he slipped through the kitchen door just as the meal was about to be served. My grandmother dropped the dinner.

When I was 6, "uncle" Art took me to the movie "King Solomon's Mines." In the dark he told me what the drums were really saying. "*Chabwino, chuma, chuma, chuma.*" He translated for the tribesmen in the film... clicking teeth and pipe tobacco breath. And when I was 16 and about to set out on the trip to Europe, a young man on his first adventure alone, Art's advice was; "Let them buy you a drink Bob, but don't let them take you upstairs."

He was 72. I had no idea who Art really was. I never asked. "Uncle Art could you really tell me about that night when you were shot? Tell me of the camels and pyramids? Did "Lawrence of Arabia" really pass through your lines at midnight? Did you kill men?"

Start at the beginning. Letters. Art was the first of the five brothers to go over. October 1914, Art's 20. Canada has just declared war on Germany. The Germans had decided to use neutral Belgium as the route to crush France in a lightning war. Britain had a pact with "poor little" Belgium. But the British small professional army didn't seem to alarm the German military planners. At the thought of the British army crossing the channel, one German General said, "If the British land, we'll arrest them." Since Britain was involved, and since civilization was threatened, Canadian boys rushed over for the big fight. War is necessary! War is an adventure! The campaigns will be heroic... and it will all be over by Christmas!!

ART "December 5th. Dear Mother,
Your letter received with much rejoicing. I have

left my sword with Aunt Isobel and have said goodbye to beds till after the war. We are now in Belgium. They didn't lose much time. We left the rest camp at Rouen on the one night and were in the trenches the next."

The first war landscape appears.

"They brought us up to the trenches about 4 o'clock one morning and the first most of us saw of the war we were picking our way over dead Frenchmen. It certainly wasn't much fun. They had been laying there three weeks. Everything has been quiet here lately. We get shelled and they get shelled a bit. A lot of sniping goes on. The trenches here are only about 39 yds. apart. Only the other night a German soldier called over in good English, 'Will you surrender?' One of our fellows replied, 'No, we won't, you fiddle faced****.' It was an experience to hear that tommy swear. If it wasn't for the funny things I think we would all go crazy."

Actor enters the trench and encounters the earth for the first time.

"To get water to drink we have to skip out at night and scoop it from the holes made by the Jack Johnsons, of course we have to boil it all."

MAN There are three German artillery sounds that we might become acquainted with, "The Whiz-bang," "The Coal Box" so named because of the black smoke given off on detonation, and the "Jack Johnson."

Sounds are provided. Actor disappears in trench on the explosion. When all is clear, he reappears with a windup gramophone. From this point on all letters are performed.

ART "The Germans have a gramophone in their trench, and they give us a concert. One of their records is 'It's a Long Way To Tipperary.' So far

I haven't plugged anyone and never shall unless it is absolutely necessary. When we are in the trenches we hardly get any sleep, on the jump the whole time. The night before we came out, it rained and the trenches surely were a little bit of hell. Over our knees in freezing muck. One gets so damned miserable that one doesn't care. We sing, tell stories, laugh and forget. Tell everyone to write as it certainly is fine to get letters out here. Love to all moth, my rose of the world. Your loving son, Art."

MAN These early letters from Art come as the German invasion had finally been halted just outside of Paris. The German army could just see the lights of Paris at night. They were then pushed part-way back. The winter began. The movement stopped. The armies dug in and the war became a monster... a three year stand-off punctuated with killing on a scale never seen before – 1915, 1916, 1917. The Generals it seemed, had a hard time learning. Too many remained in the past. For too many the world remained flat. The French army still wore red pants to battle, the British army had yet to think of steel helmets, and the Germans still wore the *Pickelhaube*, that little leather helmet with the little "pik" on top. The little pik was there to deflect the enemies sword as he cut down on your head. What's hard to imagine is Private Adolf Hitler wearing the *Pickelhaube*. He did though. He was in the 6th Bavarian division in the Ypres area the same time as Art and a number of my uncles. So he too must have been "pickelhaubed." Inscribed on Adolf's German army belt buckle was *Gott Mit Uns* – God With Us. But Adolf was the future as was the machine gun. The machine gun was unbeatable and the German machine guns mowed men down. Did the allied Generals change tactics? They persisted with the "human wave" method, the massed frontal assault. And waves of our infantry were mowed down. Our cavalry was mowed down. But even in 1915, the British General Douglas Haig said "The machine gun is a much overrated weapon, two per battalion is more than sufficient." He was soon made Commander-in-Chief.

ART "All around us is ruin, the farms are deserted. The crops are laying on the ground. At present it is all trench work. A lot of sniping goes on. However, one gets used to it. I used to duck. I don't duck now (often). The German guns make an awful racket. I've seen a hole made by 'Jack Johnson' 25 feet deep."

Artillery sounds continue at a distance until the silence of Christmas day.

"For curiosity we weighed an overcoat just out of the trenches, it weighed nine pounds when it went in, and 135 when it came out—it hardly seems possible—water and mud. Northern Belgium is like Holland, very close to sea level and drainage is essential if you want anything solid to walk on. Send artillery shells into very wet ground and what do you get?

"The weather is terrible for this kind of work. Rain every day and a frost at night. I feel the damp cold more than I ever did in Canada. The men are very cheerful considering they have to spend their Christmas over here. I haven't much to ask for. Every night each man gets a big drop of rum, and you just bet I take my share - I'd have been in hospital long ago if I hadn't."

The carol "Stille Nacht" *is heard. The first Christmas table is created.*

"Well Moth, Christmas is coming soon. Give my love to all and wish them a Merry Christmas for me. Art."

MAN There were strange stories circulated in the first months of "The Great War": Angels and Spirit-Bowmen had been seen over the battle of Mons; a Canadian soldier had been crucified by the Germans using bayonets instead of nails. But fever infects many a brain during war and not many strange stories turned out to be true. But one was. And Art was there.

ART "I was walking back on Christmas Eve with the officer of the half company we had relieved. We stopped in the barnyard of a farm while he told me the details of the trenches. Everything was smashed around us, the barn was still smouldering, smells and dirt around were terrible. I happened to ask him the time. Five after twelve on Christmas Eve. We started to laugh. 'Merry Christmas' said I, 'The same to you but never in a place like this again.' Everything was perfectly quiet until the morning. Not a shot was fired.

"About noon Christmas Day one of the Germans, they can nearly all speak English, shouted over 'Merry Christmas' and of course we shouted back, 'Merry Christmas.' 'Come over here' one of them called. 'You come over here' we answered. 'We'll come halfway if you come the other half,' replied the German. So a couple of our men stood up in the trench and the Germans did the same. Pretty soon we were scrambling towards one another, without rifles of course, and we met half way. Both sides were a little shy at first but we soon warmed up and shook hands and laughed and joked. Soon one of them said, 'You sing us a song and we'll sing you one.' So we gave them 'Tipperary' which they enjoyed very much."

German portraits have appeared and we take time for the German soldiers choir.

"They sang us a couple of songs, I don't know what they were but they sounded all right. It was rather an experience.

"The Germans told our men frankly that they didn't mind charging the French, but they charged our lines, 'with much less gusto.' The men had a huge time with the Germans and all were mighty sorry when dusk began to fall and we thought it time to get back to our lines. All this rather helped pass away the day out here. We had great fires in the trenches and spent the remainder of the evening singing. The Germans told us they were very fed up with the war.

"I did get mournful a couple of times on Christmas, I just couldn't help it when I thought of how far I was from home and my loved ones, Oh mush."

Actor lies back and drifts to childhood. He hears what the child hears from the adult conversation downstairs. Actor lies in bed happy to shoot his toy soldiers. His six-year-old monologue is recorded.

BOY I hear voices from downstairs. I am six and I have to stay at my grandmother's house. I think Uncle Art is snoring again. There's that light in the hall. I'll just lie and watch it. He took me to the movies today and told me what the tom-toms were saying... *chabwino, Chuma, chuma, chuma, Chuma, chuma, chuma*. The good part of being sent to my Gran's are my soldiers. They come in boxes from the basement. They're from an old war. Uncle Art's bullet is from that war.

ART's recorded voice is now heard. The soldier's creed "if there's a bullet made for you, you'll get it, and when in doubt, drink rum."

His teeth come out. I think that is who is telling stories downstairs. Just leave a space to see the light out in the hall. I'll sleep like a soldier. "Alice is marrying one of the guards, A soldiers life is terrible hard."

ART's letter again recorded, very informal, just the thoughts and the breaths from inside. Projections take us into the child's imagination. We gradually enter into the sound world of that night, rain, voices, artillery, soft singing, motors. Eventually the actor enters into the world of the projections.

German Soldiers

ART "The weather had taken a turn for the worse. Rain and lots of it. It made the trenches damnable. In the opposite trench a German had an umbrella and he was very nervous for fear our lads would shoot a hole in it. So he called across to us, 'Please, not to shoot holes in it as it was only an umbrella.' And he held it up at arms length to show us. 'Please, not to shoot holes.' Very funny to see this umbrella bobbing down the trench.

"It's funny how many bullets can go near one without making connections. A long string of men across a field, and bullets were plopping all over the shop and not a man got hit. It's all luck anyhow.

"The Allemand copped me at last. A damned silly way to get plugged too. I was hit while in an ambulance. I caught a chill in the trenches and the Doc thought I'd best go back to Ypres for a couple of days. It was pitch black and raining heavily. The ambulances were on the road outside the Chateau about 3/4 of a mile behind the trenches. One could just make out the dim forms of men all wending their way. Scarcely a word was spoken, only the slog of boots in the mud and the sound of the rain. Now and then a moan escaped as a stretcher bearer stumbled in the darkness.

"The whines of 'strays' had increased. There was a scream a short way ahead followed by the splash of a body falling in the mud. Hurrying up I saw a small group of men kneeling, engaged in taking off the man's equipment, his coat open showing a wound in his chest. A glance was enough to see that 'Poor Bill' was beyond human aid. He was left to be carried to the graveyard with its pathetic row of wooden crosses.

"The ambulances were busy loading. Everyone was getting a little more cheerful. I was invited by the driver of the rear ambulance up on the front seat with him. The district around here is pretty well wooded, and there are a couple of

Allemand snipers loose inside our lines. The driver was evidently anxious to get off. He showed me numerous holes in the ambulance, drilled by bullets – close shaves.

"Well it was one of these swine I let drive. Someone shouted and I felt a thud in my back which threw me forward in the dashboard. The bullet came through the rear of the ambulance and got me. It was just like someone hitting me suddenly with a hammer.

"It numbed me. All I could do was lie back in the seat and hate the Germans. The driver said I could hate very well for an officer. We started for Ypres. How that driver saw in the darkness was marvel to me. Every few minutes he called out like the blast of a foghorn 'ambulance coming, keep to the right'."

Ambulance motors recede. Pause. The dream is broken.

MAN I went back to Belgium. When I read this letter I had to find the place where Art was hit. I had to walk in his footsteps. Why? I don't know why. Who can answer these questions? And I realized that I would have to do it at night because that was Art's experience of it. He was marched into the line at night, taken out of the line at night. For a fighting soldier darkness was part of his working life. It was by night that all the surface movement took place. Food, mail, rum rations were brought up in sand bags. It was the time to evacuate the wounded, and collect the dead. It was at night and in the rain. In Art's time in the trenches, of 136 days and nights, it rained for 118 of them.

So that was how I had to find it... using an old military map, a Dutch book about Chateau's, Art's letter, and the enthusiasm of two Flemish men at the documentation centre in Ypres. I felt excitement and sadness all at once... there's the road to Ypres, the Chateau which Art mentioned,

"Kasteel Palingbeek"—rubble by 1916—would have been where that cemetery is now. The Chateau had been taken over and used as a field hospital. Those who could not be saved were hastily buried in the Chateau grounds. So Old Bill's remains would lie right there. A wood. Another wood. Do I hear a sniper? And just north, a dark smudge on the horizon the town of Ypres, in the process of being reduced to brick dust. I stand in the wet darkness, I actually stand here... with Art. The rain. The mud. The night. I feel as if I am watching history with my skin.

A Charles Chaplin romance is heard. JOE's attestation paper. The Attestation questions are recorded. The actor responds in character. JOE's projection appears.

What is your name?
"Joseph Benjamin Stratford."
In what town, township or Parish were you born?
"Brantford, Ontario."
What is the name of your next-of-kin?
"My Mother is Mrs. Elizabeth Stratford."
What is your date of birth?
"June 13th 1889. I am 25."
What is your trade or calling?
"Gentleman."
Married?
"No."
Willing to be vaccinated?
"Yes."
Have you served in any active Militia?
"Dufferin Rifles."
Height?
"5′11."
Complexion?
"Fair."
Eyes?
"Light brown."
Hair?
"Brown."

Joseph Stratford

I consider him fit – he can see the required distance with either eye; his heart and lungs are healthy, he has the free use of his joints and limbs, and he declares that he is not subject to fits of any description.

Are you willing to be attested to serve in the Canadian Over-Seas Expeditionary Force?

The Chaplin romance is JOE's theme. JOE's coat is his girl. The trunk is his horse.

JOE "Dearest Mother,
I keep both my own horses busy all day just on the gallop from morning till night. One of them is a beaut. She can go like grease lightning and turn in her own length. She has got more brains than a man.

"There is only one complaint and that is that our Cavalry unit is not at the front. Though there's word that we are to be in an Indian Army Division which includes the Bengal Lancers (supposedly the finest Cavalry in the world). They carry the lance as well as the sword and we may have to do the same later on. There is to be an army of 50,000 mounted men at the front when the spring drive takes place. Now all we have to pray for is a charge and of all the glorious things that will ever be pulled off in this world, it will be the best. Can anyone imagine 50,000 in a Cavalry charge? It just makes my hair curl to think of it. Well Moth, I would have much rather stayed in Ireland the people were so hospitable. Oh my, talk about pretty girls, there are twenty in Ireland to every one in England. At Canterbury we can hear the roar of the big guns. I do wish they would drop us in France or Belgium. I am crazy to get there. Heaps of love and lots to yourself, Your loving son Joe.
P.S. This is a quill pen, how do you like it?

"Dearest Mum,
Talk about Queens, you should see the half dozen

I have eating out of my hand just now. One is the daughter of a man who has 2000 acres, another is the daughter of a widow with about 100,000 quid per year. I really think I will have to bring one home with me, just to show the girls at home where they get off at and to let them know they can't play fast and loose with me. You should just see the 2000 acres' one, rosy cheeks, beautiful, a dream of about twenty summers. Her family keeps a butler but I am so accustomed to them now that I don't shake hands with them when they open the door. Won't it be wonderful when I get home again. We will be able to sit around the fireplace and talk all night, and the most interesting part is yet to come although the past just seems almost like a dream or some book I have read.

"I must stop all this foolish talk about the Queens and get into bed as I am turning out at 6 these mornings. Well dearest don't worry as I think the end of the war is not far off.

"So far its been like one big picnic and I can't see how it's going to be anything else. Write soon and a good long newsy letter. Tell Rick to write. What's the matter with him? Rick hasn't written a scratch since I came away.
Love to all and heaps for yourself. Joe."

Gas shells and concussion. Ringing of the gas bells.

MAN Poison gas was first used by the Greeks in the Wars of the Peloponnese around 410 BC. The Germans improved the chemistry and reintroduced it April 22nd 1915 around five in the afternoon. The gas was "improved" by Professor Fritz Haber in Berlin. Fritz Haber was a "good colleague" of Albert Einstein. These two scientists at the same institute pulled the world in opposite directions at the same time. 160 tons of Haber's chlorine gas came in a three-metre-high fog, greenish yellow, rolling over the front.

Canadians were among the first to breathe it. But they made a stand and held the line. Of the 5000 dead, 2000 were Canadian. There were no gas masks. Many Canadians found they could continue fighting by tying cloth soaked in their urine over their faces. The reputation of the Canadians soared.

Punch cartoon acknowledging the Canadian fighting at Ypres.

JOE "Moth,
Just didn't our Johnnie Canucks show them how to fight. They made the greatest stand that any army has ever made in the history of the world. And the English people are just commencing to realize and appreciate what Canada is doing for them. Yesterday day we rode with our company into an old gents estate and asked him if we could ride our men through his deer park and over his fields and he said 'certainly not, cutting up his meadows and frightening the deer,' but when he found out later that we were Canadians, 'My dear boy, you can ride your men through my house if you want to, go any place that you like, the place is yours.'

"Arthur was discharged from hospital. He says he'll have to keep his bullet. He is looking and feeling fine. There was a real little Queen in for tea on Sunday and Art and I had quite a fight about who was going to have her. I don't care who gets her as long as she is in the family. She has simply oodles of money and she is real Scotch from Edinburgh.

"This is a delightful place, I just can't help going down to the beach and watch the millions of Queens in swimming. This place would just suit Ed Osborne because all the girls wear those skin-tight bathing suits just like men. Oh my, some girls too! Everything is rosy and we are enjoying ourselves at everything but war.

Canada! Ypres: April 22-24, 1915

"Ten of the officers from our mess in the last week have gone to France and I do hope my turn will come soon.
Give my love to everyone. Hugs and kisses for yourself. Your loving son, Joe.
P.S. The strawberries are lovely over here now."

Projection of GEORGE. His music. The "Attestor" is again recorded less polite than last time.

What is your name?
"George Stratford."
In what Town, Township or Parish were you born?
"Brantford, Ontario."
What is the name of your next-of-kin?
"My Mother is Elizabeth Stratford."
What is the date of your birth?
"I am 23."
What is your trade or calling?
"Student."
Married?
"No."
Willing to be vaccinated?
"Oh yes."
Have you ever served in any Military Force?
"Ummm... Cadets."

Actor discovers his resemblance to GEORGE.

Height?
"6'1." [My height.]
Complexion?
"Fair." [My skin.]
Eyes?
"Grey Blue." [My eyes.]
Hair?
"Fair." [My hair.]
"Are you willing to be attested?"

Actor enters the barn. Firing is heard in the distance. GEORGE is beset with lice.

George Stratford

GEORGE "Things are not quite as I imagined them. It is very quiet especially in the daytime, at night the rifles crack away, a few bombs and a shell now and again. We are at present in barns. We have beds made of poles and chicken wire, and when we get blankets it's not too cold. It's just as well we do sleep a little off the floor because the rats are so numerous, this part of the country is infested. I never saw so many in my life. I woke up one night to find a great big fellow on my pillow. My boots and various parts of my equipment soon sent him flying. They are just as plentiful in the trenches. If you are on guard rats run between your feet or up and down the parapets chasing one another.

"I can't vouch for having put any Huns under the sod but I have sent a few pellets of lead over their way. I wish you could send me a couple of pairs of socks every now and then because the ones I have are wearing out. Oh yes, and some of that insect powder, for no matter where we go we have their company."

MAN Rats ran free. They had no predators. Cats were gone and nothing would keep a dog in a trench. With the amount of death about, rats had a good feed. But by this point, late 1915, the front was quieter. Major offensives would come in the spring. Still there was what the army called "wastage" which amounted to 7000 men a week lost to shells and bullets.

GEORGE "Mother more than anything else at the present moment I want a bath, we sure do get dirty and it is sometimes weeks before we can get a decent wash. If you are thinking of sending me anything, make it something good to eat like a loaf of homemade bread, and a few chunks of Mayden's fudge. There is a man in the trench who snores just like dad... and sometimes I creep along and listen to him.

"Moth, I had a bath yesterday. We were paraded to a big carpet factory, we were introduced to the dyeing vats which were full of hot water for the purpose."

The laundry workers are heard singing. The Belgian girl speaks Flemish. She has GEORGE's sock. GEORGE nods and slowly realizes that he is naked.

MAN The laundry and delousing took place at the same time as the bath, and if young Belgian women worked the laundry that day, these baths were places of double pleasure.

"He jÿ daar, zÿn jullie Canadezen? Ik heb nog nooit zulke grote kousen in mÿn leven gezien!"

The steam, the heat, hundreds of naked young men marching through in parties of fifty and the ogling in Flemish and English.

"He jÿ daar! Toon me eens hoe je die kousen aantrekt. Ben je een Engelsman? Oh, je bent Canadees. Wat is je naam? Je naam?" "George Stratford." *"Georges Stratford."* "Yes, could I have my sock back please?"

GEORGE at last covers his modesty.

GEORGE "I never enjoyed a bath so much in my life. You should see some of these billets, they are about as poor specimens of barns I ever saw. The only thing that is at all decent about them is the roof, which is made of tile and keeps out most of the rain, and the houses, they are just a continuation of the barn and are just about as bad. At present I am seated on my bed of straw in one side of our horse stall, in the centre of the floor a big brazier of soft coal is burning, and sitting around in a circle are all the boys in the depths of an argument as to how long this war is going to last. Warriors basking in the firelight. A song or two is sung and then off to bed.

My hands are getting cold, I'll have to draw near to the fire and warm them a bit before I do any more writing."

The actor leaves GEORGE suspended.

MAN A brazier?!! I haven't seen that word since I last read Shakespeare's *Henry IV Part II*. Who are these men, stragglers from the Wars of the Roses? What's changed for Private George Stratford by the brazier in a barn? There would be 200 men sleeping in the straw, straw probably soured by the previous occupants, plus the rats and lice. Sounds like Napoleons' march on Moscow. What's changed? The fact that "modern" armies now had their soldiers live and fight in holes in the ground? That the Generals thought their men should devolve to the level of killer rodents? Waiting for favourable winds for poison gas?

At the beginning of the 20th century the Generals drove the world backwards, shrinking the horizon of human behaviour. Yes they had discovered industrial techniques for killing but what were their ambitions for humanity? "Let's fight our way back to the 18th century. Let's fight our way back to the 16th century. Let's fight our way back to the 1st century if the men will let us."

I enjoy the friction of contradictions... how human endeavour can be pulled in opposite directions at the same time. There was another young man, not much older than George Stratford, who sat in an institute in Berlin and threw open the horizon of human existence.

As ALBERT is revealed he takes his place on the stool back to back with GEORGE. The actor slowly spins in place from one to the other. GEORGE's pencil is passed back and forth.

And I ask myself, how does such devolution that engulfed my "uncles," exist so precisely in time and space with such an evolution of vision and profundity? Because less than one hundred hours after my uncle George, seated by the brazier, finished this letter, finished "George" with his pencil stub, this other young man, Albert, stood up in Berlin and spoke with genius about the bedrock of our being. Albert Einstein, leapt one hundred years ahead to describe a world which even today we are slow to comprehend. What lies between the world the Generals created for George and Albert's vision? Not much time and not much space. While George's leaders were actually making military maps of the mud, a few hundred kilometres to the east, at the Kaiser Wilhelm Institute, Albert was making mathematical maps of a "reality" so profound, so far reaching that they did what Copernicus and Galileo did, propel forward consciousness of how we actually stand in the universe.

But back in the mud, my uncle George waits for the next leap backward... that as the front spasmed to a standstill, the earth in which they slept, ate, stood and fought became septic. Impossible to clear away at times, dead men dead horses, some days old, some months old, soon years old, some whole some piecemeal, became a pestilence which poisoned the earth. And George's world became an open latrine for men and horses. Rather than risk the open pits back of the lines, many men would rather shit in their helmets and throw it into "No Mans Land." If there was not time to piece together and bury all the dead, who would have time to remove the daily manure? Each division might have 6000 horses. It was said that you smelt the frontlines before you ever saw them. It was said that on a hot day the sounds of the fly's wings as they fed, could drown out the noise of approaching shells. The enemy's lead was cleaner than the earth.

> *The first of the five helmets has now been unearthed from the sand.*

Albert saw the madness. He understood devolution. He spoke of relativity and astonished those who heard him by describing the very shape of existence. But Albert's clarity and vision went beyond relativity and the new shapes that men and mud and bullets and planets and stars and galaxies make in space and time. He pointed out a humane shape for humanity. Even before Art fired his first bullet in the trenches in November 1914, Albert was circulating a counter-manifesto called "Appeal To Europeans," urging sanity and a "United States Of Europe."

Actor recreates the Christmas table. Sounds of the distant artillery to carry under combining with "Stille Nacht."

Another Christmas, the casualty lists of the next spring were yet to come. The family was still scattered this Christmas. Art was out of hospital and off with his Regiment tobogganing down stairs on overturned tables. George was at bomb school. Joe's dreams of a cavalry charge were dimming but he was still "crazy" to get into the fight. But the fourth and fifth brothers had now arrived in England, Jack and the oldest brother Harold.

Actor retrieves HAROLD's folder. It is empty. He holds the empty folder in the air and HAROLD's negative picture appears on it.

Harold's story is short. Harold's story here is silent, because while waiting in winter camp to be sent to the European mud he became ill with pleurisy, pneumonia and later TB of the lung. Harold was invalided back to Canada. His health never really recovered. He died nine years later in the sanatorium in Gravenhurst, Ontario.

L 'Histoire du Soldat. Devils Dance. JACK's projection. JACK's attestor is very blunt as is JACK.

Jack's story is anything but silent. I call Jack "the pragmatist!" He was a hunter. He was to be in more fighting than any of the others. Attestation No. 447787.

Harold Stratford

Name.
"Jack."
In what town, township or Parish were you born?
"Brantford."
What is the name of your next-of-kin?
"Mrs. Elizabeth Stratford."
Date of your Birth?
"28."
Trade or calling?
"Accountant."
Married?
"No."
Willing to be Vaccinated?
"Yes."
Have you ever served in a Military Force?
"91st Highlanders."
Do you understand the nature and terms of your engagement?
"Yes!"

MAN The brothers were ecstatic because they had finally persuaded their mother to make the voyage to Britain. And fate was kind to them since they were all in England at the time and they all got permission to see her.

My great grandmother risked the German submarine threat and arrived January 1917. She stayed with her sister Isobel and her 19-year-old niece Margaret. By now George had been wounded as well as Art. Harold was already ill. My great grandmother came at a time when the war euphoria had collapsed. Heroism was being pushed aside by cynicism. Even her sister Isobel called the casualty lists appalling. Our soldiers were, according to a German officer, "Lions led by donkeys."

MOTHER's letter is recorded, the first woman's voice in the evening. Her projection appears. The actor listens, gradually lying down in the light from the crack in the door.

All the boys revel in the fact that their mother has arrived.

Jack Stratford

MOTHER "My dearest family, it seems since ever I arrived we have been in a state of uncertainty about the boys, I told you about Harold being in London and having a month's leave on account of having an attack of pleurisy, he seems quite better and was thoroughly examined by experts and they said his lungs were perfectly all right. Joe came on Friday for four days. He is looking splendidly and quite fat. He thinks he will be off to France at the end of the week.

"While at dinner Thursday evening, a wire came saying 'Short leave arrive 9:45 PM signed Stratford.' We had a great time guessing who Stratford was, and Arthur turned up. He has changed a good deal, is a little thinner and much older looking, quite English in his quick way of speaking more than accent. Arthur is in love with going to Africa to fight.

"We were settling down for a quiet and rather lonely time when a letter came from Jack on Saturday morning and he arrived in the afternoon and has six days, I have never seen him look so well.

"George arrived as well and he looks so nice. He has not changed so much as Arthur, but he also looks older and no wonder, he has had several narrow escapes. One day he was on a wagon taking water up to the front line, another was ahead when a shell fell between the two, fortunately it was a dud... which means it did not go off."

We hear the distant sounds of the artillery from France.

"From the little things George says, he must have been in a pretty tight corner last June. They were only a handful, and when he was wounded and the Germans were only the width of the room distant and he kept on firing until his arm got so sore he couldn't hold his rifle and then he didn't get to the dressing station for three days.

Mother

Aunt Isobel and Margaret say his private's uniform didn't fit him anywhere but they loved him just the same. You would be surprised to see Aunt Isobel, the boys just treat her as they do me, and I mean pulling her about and kissing her etc. and she loves it and them, everyone. Margaret says she doesn't know which one she loves best, each one as they go she thinks it is that one, and they are all lovely to her.

"George and Margaret are trying to build a large cage for a pair of parakeets which Margaret has and loves."

The bombardment grows. The actor enters the memory, extinguishing all candles as the bombardment intensifies.

"It is very quiet and hard to realize I am any nearer the war. The nurses here say that word has been sent to have 1,000,000 beds ready for the big push in the spring, doesn't it seem awful? How little we can see into the future. They say they are sending every available man over very soon. Everyone seems to think there is going to be an awful fight. It makes me shudder to think what a terrible slaughter it means.

"Now I have seen all the boys I have to depend upon letters. I am getting pretty homesick to hear from anyone. I wonder when I will see you all again and what will have happened in the meantime. It makes me tremble to think sometimes."

The rest of MOTHER's letter becomes difficult to distinguish because it is only one of many voices of the bombardment.

"There are lots of rumours going about, one, that there is only enough food in England for two months, another that the German fleet will come out and there will be a terrific naval battle. Aunt Isobel has decided to dig up part of her lawn and put in vegetables. I am hoping everyday for a letter and although I know I write very uninteresting letters, will answer at once. A heart full of love and God bless you everyone."

We are lost under the sounds of concussion and artillery. A mortar explodes above us. Gas alarm gongs are heard as are the screams of the dying horses.

In the disappearing light we see the actor sitting rodent-like in a gas mask under the fading projection.

Black.

The Road to Ypres.

ACT TWO

In the dark a match is struck. JACK is announced. A cigarette is lit. The whispers of night sounds are heard. JACK's shaking is pronounced. The Road to Ypres is projected.

JACK "It was then about 3:30 AM and we were to go over about 4:30 AM so believe me I did some tall thinking in that hour. It isn't the chances or excitement that gets your nerve, but it's the waiting. I got in-between two old men, and in a few minutes word was passed along to fix bayonets and put 5 rounds in the magazine. Well I shook a little but nevertheless I got the bayonet in and 10 rounds in the magazine and one in the breach, and a few minutes later, at 4:30 sharp our artillery opened up a barrage raising 100 yds after every 5 minutes."

The artillery is ever-present.

"After 7 minutes we got word to go up and go over, which we did, not according to my idea of a charge though. I thought we would strip down and go over with a dash and a shout, but we didn't. We were fully clothed and equipped with 120 rounds of ammunition, rifles, bayonet, entrenching tool, pack, sand bags, shovel, 48 hours' rations and numerous sundries, and we got up with our rifles slung over our backs and walked across 1200 yards of hissing hell, dropping at intervals into shell holes to get our wind, and it just took us about an hour to make Fritz's front line. It seemed a week to me. He made it a hell-hole for us to go through. I got over to within about 30 yards of Fritz's front line when I spies a Fritz with a machine gun in a piece of trench which hadn't been cleared and about the same time he saw me, so I jumped for a shell hole and made it, the fellow coming up behind me jumped too, but not quick enough as he came into the same hole stone dead shot right between the eyes. That Fritz with a few others who had been missed kept us in that shell hole for about 30 minutes but eventually we bombed his soul to — and went on over. Within the next few hours we had taken two villages and gone over to about 100 yards behind Fritz's support trench, which we held. The hand to hand fighting is what I like, but I've been disappointed in one thing, I couldn't get satisfaction for Aunt Isobel, Fritz won't face the bayonet, and I hadn't the heart to stick it in when he had his hands up. I myself in one village took eight, 2 officers and 6 men, searched them and sent them back. One of them was an Iron Cross man, I took the ribbon off him but have since lost it.

"Their artillery started in hammer and tongs and we just sat and shook, and that afternoon Fritz got really mad. First he knocked the wind out of me 3 or 4 times, concussion, then when I was moving down the trench he rapped me on the elbow with a piece of shell casing, so I put back to my hole, then he dropped a big one right back of me and blew me right out of the trench, but I crawled back again and a few minutes later I got a bump back of the ear, just under my tin roof, and thank the Lord it wasn't coming any faster than it was or I wouldn't be here now.

"I never was so glad to get out of any place before in my life, and I never stopped shaking until last night. I was steady enough going over, and while we were scrapping, as a matter of fact I stopped on the way over and lit a cigarette and went on, but lying in a hole and being shelled sure gets you, I couldn't have lit a cigarette then to save my soul, I was shaking too badly.

"Don't worry about me, I'll be all right. I'm lucky, I can see that.
Lovingly, Jack."

Detonator marker. Actor stands with bayonet in hand, it becomes his "Vigil" sword.

MAN "Challenge and Response." The vigil, I remember it now, "Do you, with this sword, accept witness of... I pledge myself to.... Then pass. And may you go with courage, vigilance and a clear heart."

A vignette. The actor's precis of the four boys punctuated by the ring of the gas gong and detonator. Each of their pictures appears.

GEORGE "Moth, will you please send a couple of pairs of socks. Don't send them too fast. A pair every week or ten days. I'll tell you when to stop... George."

JOE "Question: Do you know which side of a horse a cavalry man gets down off? Answer. He doesn't get down off either side, he gets down off a duck. Joe."

ART "Mother... pass on to the boys at home if you would; *Mukhale ime ni moya nthami zones ndi umpulumutsa chuma chuma chuma*... Art."

JACK "Moth... the parcel arrived with the 'vermin vest.' Some shirt I say, eh what? I'd like to know though what the smell is for, is it to drive the animals from my person or to attract them on to my shirt? I don't know if I'll be able to stand it or not without my gas mask on... Jack."

GEORGE "Mum... the last socks you sent were fine and I could do with another pair when you get the time to do them for me..."

JACK "Moth please, if its not too much trouble will you send me a few moth balls. I'm going to try a new experiment on Mr. Louse..."

JOE "It was a beautiful warm afternoon so another chap and myself went down to the beach and lay in the sun and then went into a pastry shop across the road and had cocoa and ate cream puffs, until we could hardly waddle back to the street car. What a life? Who wouldn't want to come to war? I am rather ashamed to tell of the good times we have. P.S. What is that little brother of mine doing these days? Rick hasn't written me a word and it's on for almost two years since I left home. Please tell Rick to wake up..."

GEORGE "Moth, I suppose they will notify you that I am in hospital but don't worry because I'm not sick enough to be here..."

Finally the actor stops the vignette.

MAN How much do you want your mother to know?

Detonator marker.

GEORGE "I thought my feet would last. But when I struck these cobblestone roads four days in succession, why they went back on me so here I am."

MAN George is in hospital for his feet? I was looking through Casualty Forms when I found it. Common diseases multiplied in the trenches. Army Form B.213, Stratford, George.

30-4-17	Joined 3rd Cdn. Ent. Battn.
6-5-17	Evacuated to Hospital (V.D.) Not Stated, Gonorrhea.
8-5-17	V.D.S. Transferred to No.39 Gen H.P.
21-6-17	V.D.G. Discharged

George, seven weeks with syphilis and gonorrhea... and there were no antibiotics in 1917. The treatment was mercury, arsenic and what was called "the hot umbrella." Ouch. Side effects: extreme local pain, renal bleeding, jaundice and death. Oh dear Mother.

The actor now begins to realize how much is hidden from him in the letters.

The first level of deception in these letters is the triviality, the off-handedness. There was so much they could not write about. It takes someone as forthright as Jack to say, "there's very little I can tell you Moth, or at least very little that I can write about." The next level of deception is the nature of the deaths. But of course, why would anyone tell a mother how horrible some of the deaths were? "He was killed instantly" was a well-worn phrase. Then there is the simplest kind of deception. In his hospital bed with syphilis George again writes his mother.

GEORGE "I went up for my final medical board and I was so hard of hearing that the doctor said I'd better take a few more weeks and have my ears attended to, so here I still am."

The actor addresses his dead relative.

MAN "Liar." And why not? What would you write your mother? As if this war were not bad enough. As if the Canadians weren't known for having the highest rates of venereal disease of everyone in Europe. I wonder if he had any scarring from the syphilis?

"Well what was it George, a bit of grumble and grunt? A bit of jiggy-jig?" How deep did my uncles have to bury their humanity to survive? Bury their desire to be loved. The 'suicide list' as Art called the lists of men destined for the front. "Did you tell Joe? I know he saw you in hospital. How did you hide the sores when the 'rooster' was inspected on dangle parade? Dangle parade? Don't pretend you don't know what the dangle parade was George. The 'short arm' inspection!"

Perspective. Perspective. Hospital admissions 1917, unrelated to enemy action; anthrax 8, dysentery 6,025, tuberculosis 1,668, venereal disease 48,507.

48,508. "At least did you have a decent time with her? Or was it 10Fr for five minutes, pants up and get out? Buttoning yourself up as you passed the line of men on the street all waiting their turn?

Help me George. You were on leave in London a month before, was she English? Was it anyone I would have read about in the letters?

"Perhaps it wasn't the Belgian girl from the laundry? Perhaps she found you returning from the front at the railway station in London... a woman whose life... who knows what her loss was... and there you were, George Stratford still muddy, aged before your time but with 10 days leave and then... there's nothing in the letters George, nothing. It's a world unspoken."

Actor has reached a dead end. He passes the letter to GEORGE. GEORGE glances at it and crumples it up in silence, pitching it back into the trench. The actor searches the earth.

This is a H.E. detonator head from the war. I bought it in Belgium for about $4.00. The frost pushed this remnant to the surface of the fields several springs ago. It's called the Iron Harvest. But when I walked in the fields it looked peaceful to my immediate eye. Peace and order were what I saw but they were just a small part of the story. The larger part of the story was that everything beneath my feet was moving. Through seasons of rain and heaving frosts, bits of rifle, detonators, barbed wire, helmets, artillery shells are slowly being pushed to the surface. There are a quarter of a million tons of unexploded shells still buried in the fields of Belgium. They will continue to surface for centuries. The larger story is that the earth is not at peace. The earth is reworking its memory of the war.

The actor falls into the dance of the skeletons. The long-dead appear with him on the scrims.

The larger story is also the dance of the dead soldiers. A hundred thousand skeletons lie unclaimed beneath the surface of the battlefields. They too are moving. Their bones dance... ever so slowly in the shifting of earth and mud...

stepping with the frosts for more than eighty years. And as the dead men dance the decades away... a few break company each spring and come to the surface... to be claimed along with the detonators and rusted helmets and finally taken to their graves. Up to 40 of these forgotten soldiers appear each year... and the other thousands return to their dance. That is the larger story. That story was never told me by my senses.

My senses are veiled. It's as if I'm only allowed to see and hear as much of the world as my mind can bear. I'm only allowed to see and hear as much of the world as is comfortable. But the dance beneath my feet in the darkness of the earth is a greater story. Above my head is a greater story... the light dance of the stars and galaxies. The worlds unspoken in my uncle's letters is the greater story.

My senses are veils. But that's the design it seems. I wasn't designed to see the dancing soldiers in the earth or the stars in the daylight sky. I certainly wasn't designed to see dark matter and black holes out there. I wasn't even designed to experience the earth as round. Really. Left to my immediate senses, there is nothing to tell me that the earth is round. The earth is flat ladies and gentleman. Sorry but every bit of evidence that I see first hand, says it's flat as a table. Don't mention pictures and don't mention technology, they are not first-hand. My senses as designed told me only of a flat world.

Because of Galileo I know the larger story that the earth is round, and because of sailors who kept not falling off the edge. But none of us knows the roundness first hand. Water does not lie in hills. Well it does. Water lies in hills. But apparently it takes more than eyes to see it. It takes a suspension of what we believe makes sense. And surely it takes courage to see the larger story beyond the comfortable ideas. And just as Galileo saw the larger story in 1610, and put us on a ball floating in space... a dizzying prospect for his Pope who was not yet ready for it – so too did Einstein in 1915 read the larger story of relativity... a dizzying prospect of curving space-time. And when will any of us be ready to "know" that great, great story relativity... perplexing and mystifying... the story conceived at the birth of the universe, the supreme contract between matter and energy, a story that says there can never be an absolute to physical existence.

At 16 I was like Galileo's Pope. I knelt through my vigil in that battle-chapel too sleepy to know that my uncles were buried close by. I stood on the edge of the battlefields not seeing that George was possibly dancing beneath that earth. Yet we will see. The great story will eventually emerge – like the memories of the fields, like the vigil of my youth, like the roundness of the earth, and like this detonator.

The detonator is lobbed back into the earth. An explosion marks it's entry. The actor is left with a single louse in his hand. Moving to silent film music, the actor side steps across to GEORGE who has been sitting quietly in the meantime.

George, how do you race a louse?

GEORGE "German dugouts are the dirtiest places in the world and as a result everybody got crumby. Well we were playing bridge in one not long ago, many feet below the ground and we had played until everyone was sick of the sight of cards and still had seven or eight hours to put in, so someone suggested that we each catch a louse, put five francs on him, lay a race course out on the table with matches, and run him over the course. It took us about an hour and a half to run the race, my horse would persist in going in the wrong direction. I don't believe I've laughed so much in ages."

The gramophone is wound. The louse is raced. MOTHER's face appears in projection. GEORGE addresses his mother.

"Mother it was funny the other night when we were in the front line, there was a nightingale, the first one I've heard in what was left of a bit of woods between the two lines. Although it was anything but quiet with rifles and machine guns cracking away, bombs and trench mortars, that bird sang incessantly the whole night through. It didn't appreciate the value of wings or it wouldn't have been where it was."

The artillery returns. For the first time GEORGE finds it difficult to speak. He knows now how much he can't say to his MOTHER.

"I've been able to see Jack a number of times, but it's only chance. As for Joe I don't see anything of him and really don't know just where he is. Our trips in the line haven't been so bad lately, although they are quite bad enough."

MAN Is this all you can say George? You are fighting the battle of Passchendaele. Is that all you can say? The battle lasted three months. By the end of it all the Canadians, George among them, had taken the remains of what was the town called Passchendaele. "Slaughter on a gigantic scale." according to Winston Churchill. For each metre gained 35 men were lost. That is one son per inch... and so little said Geordie. To prepare for the battle, horses and tractors had positioned one piece of heavy artillery every six metres for 25 kilometres. The bombardment was continuous for a week. That week reduced the fields to a diarrhea of mud and slime. I try to imagine what it would be like to drown in it, because they did. I try to imagine drowning in mud at night. At least Geordie, you managed to write, "This Belgium mud is something fierce." The British command had been warned off this kind of bombardment because of the battle conditions it would produce. Only after did a British Chief of Staff visit the battlefield. It was reported that he wept. It was reported he said, "Good God, did we really send men to fight in that?" The reply was, "It's worse further on up". 15,654 Canadians were killed, missing or wounded.

GEORGE "Mother, in one place the two lines were so close together that you had to stand all night with your revolver in one hand and a Mill's bomb in the other. Fritz did try to come over a number of times but what with bombs, rifle grenades and rifle bullets he didn't get very far.

"It's one of those clear, cool glorious days where if you look heavenward there's nothing to remind you there's a war on at all except a few small puffs of anti-aircraft shells, but you can't keep looking heavenward all day and your gaze comes down to earth again and then it all comes back with a big thud. Here I am again back in the midst of the Flanders mud."

Actor points to where GEORGE was standing.

MAN 15,655.

GEORGE "I'm about all that's left in the way of officers in this Company so you can imagine we have a pretty tough time, however we were right there with the goods as usual."

Ghosting in is the projection of the Night Letter informing GEORGE's mother of his death.

"Spending leave at Aunt Isobel's, believe me it's good to have a place like that to go to, otherwise I don't know how I'd manage as well. Margaret and Aunt Isobel both well. Margaret and I took in a roller rink a number of times and the movies every afternoon. She looks stronger I think every time I see her."

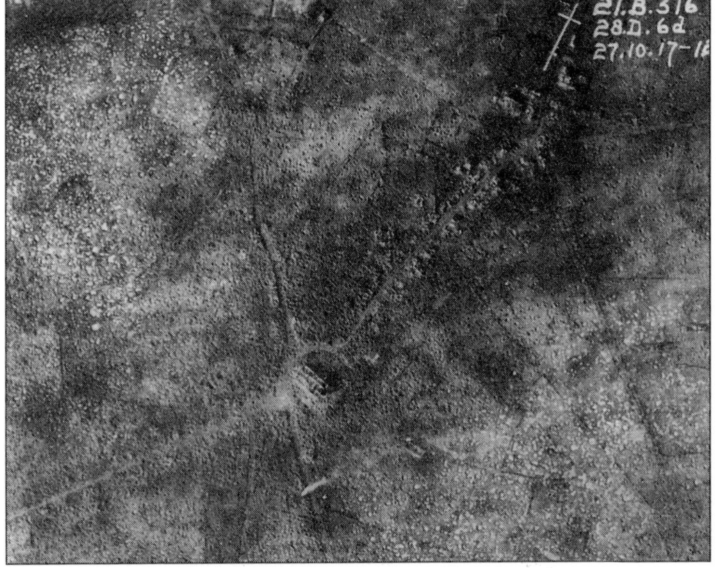

The town of Passchendaele before and after the battle of 1917.

The actor now stands with his death notice projected on him.

"The Belgium mud is something fierce. You absolutely can't stir out of your billet without getting plastered with it. That was a fine letter I got from you some time ago, I hope you come across with another soon. We expect to go up the line for a day or so and then back for a good old rest which we Greatly need.
Heaps of love and to everyone at home.
Your loving son,
George."

Silence. Night Letter is now heard in recording.

OFFICER Night Letter from Great Northern Western Telegraph Co. Mrs. Joseph Stratford, Idlewyld, 4460 deeply regret to inform you Lt George Stacy Stratford infantry officially reported killed in action November seventeenth nineteen seventeen. 817AM Director of Records.

Actor searches for next letter from the boy's files placed about the stage. Finds JACK.

JACK "Have just returned from a visit to George's unit where I found out about poor old Geordie. It seems pretty rotten luck, as Capt. Little put it, that he should go so far and then get it where and when he did. They had been up in the line three days and been through one of the worst bombardments they had ever experienced and everything went fine and things were comparatively quiet. About an hour before they were to be relieved, George was up on top arranging guides for the relief, when a whiz-bang came over and got him, and he was killed instantly, which is something to be thankful for, as I would hate to think he had been wounded and probably buried alive in the mud.

The conditions were such that they were unable to bring his body out, so they buried him just back of the line. Everyone I spoke to had a good word to say for poor old Geordie.

"Capt. Little asked me to come over and have dinner with him and the officers who were with Geordie the night that he was killed. But I don't think I'll go, it's bad enough over here as it is, and everybody is kept pretty busy thinking about themselves, so I don't think I'll bother these fellows. They are all strangers to me.

"The exposure and suffering here would make your blood run cold, and in lots of cases where the wounded are unable to get out themselves, they lay in the mud and eventually die of exposure. Thank God that poor Geordie didn't get any of that. Considering everything we have been pretty lucky to get through this far without getting worse than we have. I only wish I could have got it instead of Geordie..."

An artillery shell explodes, far too close. JACK's letter is dropped. The actor searches GEORGE's file.

MAN Isobel's daughter Margaret was heartbroken according to her mother. Margaret exists in only one letter which she writes to George's mother, who by this time had returned home to Canada.

The photograph of MARGARET Osbourne is projected. Her letter is recorded and spoken as if in natural dialogue. Important that the recording includes the laughter of this young woman.

MARGARET "Dear Aunt Elizabeth.... You asked me to tell you about dear old Geordie's last leave. I remembered he wired us the time he would arrive, 4:45 I think, and after lunch Mother and I started walking downtown but about half way, it being rather cold I had to turn back as I felt wheezy, and I had not been in the house three minutes when didn't George arrive on an earlier train. It was just as if I had come back to meet him, strange wasn't it?

and then of course my wheeze departed as it usually does when any of the boys arrive. You don't know the difference their coming has made to me, not only making me forget that I can't breathe but making me happy.

"We went to quite a few movies at the Electric theatre and Mother kept turning around every six steps and saying, 'Aren't you coming?' and every time Geordie would stick his head forward and grin like Charlie Chaplin, than pull it back again quickly – you know the way, and oh! it was funny! and he used to do it when we played Rum, and now I can't help thinking of him every time we play."

Actor has been absorbed in MARGARET's letter.

MAN I feel that if I read this letter closely enough, I might hear the last few breaths. Passing my fingers through those breaths I might touch George... Margaret. This comma, that thought, if I could peel back the pencil I might feel how he pressed this paper when he thought of Margaret. Margaret with her asthma which would bring her own premature death.

And Jack. "I only wish I could have got it instead of Geordie"... this from Jack who likes the hand-to-hand fighting best. Jack who had been over the top, shelled, gassed, concussed, wounded. Jack, was this an impulse which lasted only in the writing? I didn't understand the remark when I first read the letter. I literally didn't understand what "got it" was... it was mistyped. The original letters were handwritten but I have only the typed version of this letter. The little sister of the family Mayden typed out all her dead brother's letters in her later years. But what Mayden typed was "I only wish I could have 'for ir' instead of Geordie." I didn't understand what 'for ir' was until I looked at a keyboard. G, F, T, R. G, F, T, R. Three times in five keys Mayden's finger slipped one key to the left. Why Mayden? In the 700

Margaret

letters you typed there are few typing mistakes. Mayden, why this one? Back and back I want to go, back to press against the heart of these moments. Back to see... what?

On the scrims appear selected frames in halting images of the men of the P.P.C.L.I. marching. The actor points out his fantasy, asking for the footage to be played again and again.

I found some actual film footage of George's regiment, 1917 the P.P.C.L.I. And I thought I saw him. There, the second in the line, there. Run it again. There, the one with the moustache. Run it again. There. No, no. Stop. Stop it. Stop it! I'm sorry. I'm obsessive.

The actor moves to leave the stage, not willing to impose his obsession any longer.

My father was killed in a car accident. His station wagon left the road and rolled and rolled. He was alone. The road was absolutely straight. There was no other traffic. He died away from us all and we didn't see his body until four days after at the funeral home. After the funeral I knew I had to find it. I had to find the place. Using the police report I drove that section of Ontario highway. At each straight-away, I would get out and look for signs... tire marks, disturbances, I wasn't sure what exactly. Nothing. I would find nothing and move on, nothing again or perhaps I thought just marks in my imagination. I felt my father slipping even further away. Standing by the roadside everything was questioned, even my reason for the search. After an hour or so, I really can't remember time, on a very long straight stretch, I saw what I thought was a disturbance in the gravel. I got out. There were two distinct signs leading slowly off, over the edge and down into a wide, grassy ditch. I descended, I was confused and excited. I had no idea what I would look for. But there, lying right across the marks coming down the grass bank, was a long indentation.

Was it the length of a station wagon? In disbelief, I find embedded in the earth pieces of plastic and glass, what I presumed was a side mirror from my father's car. I knew from the report that it had rolled many times. I found a second horizontal gash, grass beaten down. Again debris embedded in the earth. Again I followed and again I found a third. What do I want to find? Why am I here? More pieces of car, this time... glass, bits of grill... and this time I'm certain because I pick out of the earth a station wagon's logo. I'm hearing sounds now. Seeing the distance between the impacts, passenger side, driver's side, passenger side, I can hear the noise and the violent clutter of the last seconds of my father's life. At first I know he was within that spinning vehicle. But I also know that in the end he was thrown free. I used what remained of my logic to imagine the last arc. Six metres away I found a small area of depressed grass. I knelt. This couldn't be where he lay... where officers stood... where a stretcher was brought... where medics' fingers pressed and listened? I press my hands to the earth. What am I going to feel, my Father's body? There pressed deep was a part of his glasses, the left half, dirt smearing the lens. I know they were his and his only because still attached was a piece of sailors twine which he used to hang them round his neck. A neck which I knew at that moment to be broken.

I've come as far as I can. I am as close to him in his last instant that I can be. I have placed my feet in his footsteps, to know him, to be there, to be here. That's all I can do. Witness.

> *Detonation. Actor returns to the reanimated footage of the marching soldiers. It finally stops and is replaced by the projected letter announcing JOE's death. The actor reads phrases from the letter with his hands as well as his voice.*

"Dear Mrs. Stratford,
It is my sad duty to inform you of the death of your son Capt. Joseph B. Stratford on the 2nd

instant. We were caught by shell fire where we were bivouacked in a wood and your son together with a number of others was unfortunately in the line of fire.

"He did not regain consciousness after he was hit and died in about fifteen minutes only. I had him carried back to a village of Dommartin and we buried him in a pretty little cemetery there. He died without having to suffer and that is the wish of all over here.
Yours Very Sincerely,
Lt-Col Paterson
Fort Garry Horse"

The voice of MOTHER spoken intimately to her son. JOE's picture is projected but this time as a negative. The actor kneels in the image.

MOTHER "My little darling son Rick, I know with what grief you will get the telegram. These are terrible times and I suppose we cannot expect to escape sacrifices, but our dear Geordie and now darling Joe seems pretty hard to hear. Our family circle is growing smaller but we must ever bring it closer together with love and helpfulness one to another. Though my heart is heavy and aching, I am well and making up my mind not to fret too much and to remember the loss is ours but theirs to gain.

"Take care of yourself dear and write often. We have had some warm weather here and in raking off the borders I find lots of perennials sticking their heads up and full of promise. The spring always makes me sure of the Resurrection and that nothing is lost.

"Now good-night with very much love and God bless you."

MAN The strangest letter of all was sent to my great grandmother from an unknown woman in France. Madame Mialaret. Joe had indeed found a "Queen," but she was not "a dream of about

Madame Mialaret

twenty summers." Joe's Queen was his second mother.

Madame's photo is projected. Her letter is recorded. The actor translates, the two voices intermingling.

"Bien chère Madame:
Vous ne savez sans doute pas que dans notre pays de France où votre cher enfant vient trouver la mort, existe une femme qui le pleure a l'égal d'un fils, et pour cause il ne m'appellait guere autrement que "maman chérie." D'abord pendant environ deux mois (1916) il fût catonné à la maison, après nous l'avons revu aussi souvent que le service lui permettait de le faire...

"You doubtless do not know that in our country of France where your dear son met his death, there lives a woman who weeps for him as a son. Indeed he would not call me anything else but '*Maman Chérie.*' At first for nearly two months in 1916, he was billeted at my house. Afterwards we saw him again. It was with us he spent his occasional days of leave. Perhaps *chère Madame* this poor child has sometimes spoken to you of me because he always promised me that after the war he would come back to see me with his '*vraie Maman.*' Alas! Fate has decided otherwise and we can only weep for the loss of one who was indeed goodness itself."

Holding up her handkerchief, the actor finds JOE's portrait projected on it.

"Dear Madame, I wish first that you should know of my existence. Also, as I only possess a very small photograph of your son, would you dear madame in the name of friendship that he has always shown me, give me a larger one that I may keep always.
In waiting,
Mme. Mialaret."

Some rousing WWI martial music here. "Here We Are, Here We Are, Here We Are Again." JACK's vignette is punctuated with recordings of his name, and a growing artillery barrage. His mother's image is present throughout.

JACK "The big feature is to forget. It's a great old war all right and sometimes it makes you wonder how you ever got through some of the places you've been in. And I'm commencing to think there's nothing more than luck on your side when you do. But that is one of the worst things you can do out here is to think, the big feature is to forget.

"Moth I went to church parade Sunday also took communion, and thought a lot about you, all day, knowing you would be going to early communion. The next day we went up the line and I did a lot of thinking that day too."

During JACK's final section, lights alter from entry to entry, treating it as pages in an ever more chaotic journal. The gas gong beats the time out as battle sounds build. The war is approaching its climax and JACK knows it.

"Moth dear the main thing is that men who give their lives in scraps, like the one Joe was in don't realize anything, but are just conscious of the roar and din of the battle, and when the end comes it is instantaneous.

"Everything is going fine here. Am enclosing four German shoulder straps, souvenirs. There is a history connected to each one and some day I'll tell you the story.

"Don't worry about the German gas old dear, it is darn uncomfortable stuff to have to put up with, but our masks are good. I'm just afraid that you will worry about me, and it makes me hate the line.

"Am sending more souvenirs. My score with the Boche is just about even.

"I wish you could see the country, not the war, it's simply beautiful. Do you remember the bush at home with the red flower? I picked some of this one day about a month ago, up in front of our support line, and took it down to decorate my dugout. Some class eh what?"

Bombardment and battle reaches crescendo. Fate has looked elsewhere and victory appears.

"Oh Lordy! Oh Lordy! you never saw anything like it in your life. I'd go back and do it over ten times through, just for the fun. This was a hell of a scrap, I was in for seven days and over the top three times. Gee I'm about the oldest man in the battalion now, and I went through the three scraps without a scratch. Pretty lucky or I miss my guess. I didn't bother much the first two scraps but that last Cambrai show I sure did think at times that my number was up. But here I am you see, all in one piece and going strong.

"I sometimes wish I could get sick and go to hospital for a rest, but I can't so there you are. I'm a healthy brute I am."

Lights momentarily on bed which is now hospital bright.

"Tomorrow will be my birthday, 31, and I guess I'll have to celebrate it in hospital. Had a go at that darn Spanish flu. The flu did me more good than harm I think, as I got a lot of gas and stuff out of my lungs and stomach."

Back to darkening battle, the cheering crowds and bands from Armistice day begin to be heard... its own martial delirium.

"Some of the most glorious weather and scrapping you can imagine. Everything went up together, smoke screen and then H.E. overhead and we walked and smoked and talked and scrapped all at one time."

By now the actor is unearthing the remaining four helmets.

"Don't worry about how I got the German shoulder straps I sent you. They are easy to get, both off the live ones and the others. One officer didn't want to give me his, but I used a little 'perswasion' and he took his knife out and cut them off for me. The 'perswasion' stuff comes from the ammunition dumps every day."

Actor is bent over object in the earth, cutting off bits of uniform, and finally stripping off belt on the buckle of which is written "Gott Mit Uns."

"You ask me if I like the Hun, or rather do I hate the Hun? Well if you want a straight answer, when you get to Heaven you ask the Hun. They are all labeled '*Gott Mit Uns*' and every time I get a chance I send them on their way to *Gott*."

Finally silence. JACK's recorded poem is played. Actor remains with bayonet and belt.

"A kiss of the sun for pardon,
The song of a bird for mirth,
You are nearer God's heart in a garden
Than anywhere else on earth."[1]

JACK drives the bayonet into the stage. One by one the boy's files are gathered.

MAN The war was over for Jack. He fought to the end. He never escaped the effects of the gas. He was in and out of the sanatorium in Gravenhurst until his death at the age of 45.

The war was over for George. He was not killed instantly as the army had said. He died in pain. His body was never found. His grave became lost in the mud of Passchendaele.

The war was over for Joe. He received the Military Cross for bravery. His body stayed in the pretty little cemetery of the village of Dommartin for 36 years until the War Graves Commission moved it to a military cemetery.

And the war was over for Harold.

The drumming of an Angoni mourning dance can be heard.

Art, the youngest who went first was last. *Mukhale ime ni moya nthami zonse ndi umpulumutsa chuma chuma chuma*. He spent almost two years with the King's African Rifles, increasingly distant from his family. Mail from home took anywhere from 3 to 4 months to reach him. He said he was rusty on what people looked like "over there." He had not recognized a photo he'd been sent of his little sister Mayden. He was the last to hear of the deaths.

ART "On Column, Nyasaland. Aunt Isobel's letter and the one from home of dear Joe's death, I received a few days ago and I really can't write my thoughts. It all seems so sudden and unreal. But all my love goes out to you Mother to help and comfort you, dearest.

"The other day one of my chaps came up and told me his brother had died, and asked permission to have a mourning dance. It was held last night in the lines. At dinner we heard the tom-toms going so we went up to see what was doing. There were three drums going as hard as the men could pound them and the dead man's next of kin were dancing about a huge fire."

The actor enters the dance.

"It was pouring rain. Around their legs they wore great bands of jingling metal and they were dancing as hard as they could in time with the tom-toms. The women were sitting round in a circle and singing. The drums were going, the men's figures lurching about in the firelight, the ringing of the metal on their legs and the song of the women.

"I woke up about midnight and as the drums were still going, I went up again to have a look. The onlookers had all gone, so had the women, the rain had put the fire out and there was only one man left dancing. The others had collapsed on the ground. The last man was about all in too but he was still shuffling about in time to the drums."

The actor awakens from his reverie. He returns the letters to the folders.

MAN It would be another year until he slipped into the men's washroom at Union Station to go Zulu, to make his sister drop the dinner. Though Chapuchapu's offer of a wife wasn't accepted, he did marry briefly after the war but his wife died in giving birth to their only child. And for reasons which have always been mysterious, Art gave that child to his youngest brother Rick... the Rick who never wrote. Art then disappeared to his life alone in northern Ontario. I wonder if it was because of what happened to George in the hospital, the V.D.S., that he advised me; "Let them buy you a drink Bob, but don't let them take you upstairs."

A detonation marker brings the actor to the letter he has always carried in his breast pocket.

The last letter. It postdates all the others, 1923. There's a flower, a mauve pansy, and a hand-drawn map, in pencil. It's of a cemetery, "August 1923, village of Dommartin Cemetery, France." This is my final guide. The young man who wrote this letter wore a fresh pansy in his lapel for the rest of his life. I remember that pansy. It's from Rick. "What is that little brother of mine doing these days? Rick hasn't written me a word and it is on for almost two years since I left home.

Please tell him to wake up." Perhaps Rick was like me when I was young though I can't believe it.

Again sounds from Le Reve.

RICK "Darling Mother, the Captain says there is still a good chance of finding Geordie's grave because nearly everyday the army is finding and identifying soldiers."

MAN 1923. They still thought they could find George's body. Rick was in Europe looking for his brother's graves for his mother. But what did he want for himself? To perform a vigil.

RICK "I can hardly describe to you the feeling I had. The presence of our soldiers seemed to fill the air. There were soldiers crowding into the trains, marching along the roads through the treeless country and yet there were no soldiers, and very few traces in the country of the war only five years ago.

"I arrived here at Dommartin this afternoon at 4 o'clock, and soon found the way to the little village cemetery which is on the outskirts of this funny old kind town. I went in through the old front gate, and to the right of me was the old kind of French cemetery, and to the left there were a row of soldiers graves. Four graves marked off into a plot and surrounded by pinks, and in the middle pansies were blooming. I stayed beside his grave for a couple of hours, Mother darling, thinking of him as he used to be, and of you, and what a wonderfully brave, uncomplaining mother you have been. I picked some pansies off Joe's grave where they were growing so beautifully, from such a precious place in France."

MAN I walked in through the cemetery gate as Rick did. I followed his footsteps to where Joe's grave had been. I stood in the farmyards with

The graves of Joe Stratford and 3 fellow Canadians, Dommartin, France.

tractors and manure to find out from the old woman if anyone remembered when the Canadian soldiers' graves had been moved. Then I had to find the Bois de Senecat. I had to find where Joe was killed.

Actor lights the candles which are in the five helmets. The officers' interjections are recorded.

OFFICER "The regiment was bivouacked for the day in the Bois de Senecat. The wood was under heavy enemy shell fire."

MAN It was not on any map. It was a farmer at the local bar who told me if I took the lane past Rouvrel, *"a gauche, a gauche,"* first I would pass a Crucifix and then further the Bois de Senecat. I asked again about the Bois de Senecat of an elderly gentleman at Rouvrel, *"Mais c'est l'histoire dur, les mortes, mais c'est l'histoire de cette pays."* I asked anyone. I asked all the questions I never asked when I was young.

It was afternoon when I found it, a patch of woods in the middle of rolling fields. The earth of the woods is still pocked marked with shell craters. Somewhere here Joe sat and was eating his lunch.

OFFICER "About 12:00 noon a group of Officers were having lunch when a H.E. shell exploded amongst them. He was killed almost outright."

MAN I walked to the east to see what the wood looked like to the men who killed him. There, breaking the surface of a field, I found German artillery shells... four of them. This is the Iron Harvest. The others I found suspicious. This one I brought home.

The actor unearths the shell casing and arranges the grave for the vigil.

OFFICER "I had him carried back to a village—Dommartin—and we buried him in a pretty little cemetery that afternoon."

MAN I must follow the body. I leave the woods by the only lane to the west to Dommartin. It must be the way. It is growing dark. I can sense my hand on the cart. Step by step I'm with Joe. It's evening by the time I returned to the cemetery.

But of course the body was moved years ago. Normand on his tractor had remembered them removing soldier's graves in 1954. Have I come as far as I can? Is my vigil finally over? I don't want to leave here, as the 16-year-old young man left his half-understood vigil. Have I "kept watch" this time?

The actor finally reclaims the sword.

The wind has picked up and for the first time in a week the night is clear. Bright and cold, they are there in their billions. In the ancient light of the universe I stand an hour over Joe's grave of 36 years. His blanket of earth pulled over him, his friends buried in the earth on either side. I know now there had been four dead soldiers in the cart.

North star over my right shoulder, the axle of the galaxy over my left, I have no further to go. I am exhilarated yet sadness is in my bones. Having come this far I now know how little of the world I see. But Albert had warned me; "Nature's only showing us the tail of the lion."

The actor lies back on the grave.

I want the great story. I want to see the body of the lion. But the light of the billions above me is part illusion. They have all moved or gone out. Even my sun and my planets are not where I see them. And while the earth and mud cling to my shoes and will claim my body as well, they have no absolute hold over me, since the earth is not absolute but the condensed energy of the light in which I live.

The music of the final dance appears.

What is absolute is the motion, lives come and lives gone. The motion is all that is left me... the turn and dance of my uncles and the stars that are no longer there yet exist just the same. And as the men dance beneath this earth so too do the stars above my head, turning this way about the pole star and that way about the galaxy.

So I can only dance, as I might have danced through the vigil of my youth, sword in hand to tell life from death, illusion from reality. And for Joe and George and Art and Jack and Harold, my dance will go on till the rains put the fires out for good. My dance will go on till I am the last brother standing. I pick a pansy off a grave from such a precious piece of earth. I have come as far as I can. I've done as much as I can. All that's left for me now is to be here.

The actor dances. He is eventually lost from sight. Blackout.

The end.

FOOTNOTE

[1] Anonymous. Found in Jack's papers after his death.

GLOSSARY

V.D.S.	Venereal Disease Syphilis
V.D.G.	Venereal Disease Gonorrhea
Cdn. Ent. Battn.	Canadian Entrenching Battallion
Gen. H.P.	General Hospital
H.E.	High Explosive
P.P.C.L.I.	Princess Patricia's Canadian Light Infantry

FLEMISH TRANSLATION

He, jÿ daar.
Hey, you there.

Zÿn jullie Canadezen?
Are you Canadians?

Ik heb nog nooit zulke grote kousen in mÿn leven gezien.
I've never seen socks this big in my life.

Toon me eens hoe je die kousen aantrekt.
Show me how to slide them on.

Ben je een Engelsman?
Are you an Englishman?

Oh, je bent Canadees.
Oh, you are Canadian.

Wat is je naam?
What is your name?

FULL TEXT OF MADAME MIALARET'S LETTER

Bien chère Madame,

Vous ne savez sans doute pas que dans notre pays de France où votre cher enfant vient trouver la mort, existe une femme qui le pleure a l'égal d'un fils, et pour cause il ne m'appelait guere autrement que "maman chérie." D'abord pendant environ deux mois (1916) il fût catonné à la maison, après nous l'avons revu aussi souvent que le service lui permettait de le faire. C'était chez nous qu'il venait passer ses permissions de quelque jours, souvent accompagné d'un ou de plusieurs camarades qui le regrettent bien aujourd'hui comme d'ailleurs, tous ceux qui l'ont connu.

Peut-être, chère Madame, ce pauvre enfant as-t-il quelque fois parlé de moi, car il aimait à me repète qu'après la guerre il reviendrait me voir avec sa vraie maman. Hélas! Le sort en à decidé autrement, et nous ne pouvons que pleurer la perte de celui qui fût la bonte même.

Nous avons revu ses camarades, son regiment est revenu cantonner à 6 kilom de la maison, les officiers n'ont pas manqué de rendre visite sur visite, et j'ai pu m'assurer que celui qui nous était cher avait reçu une sepulture dans un petit cimetière a l'arrière du front d'Amiens. J'ai tendrement embrassé, en pensant à vous, les deux officiers qui lui avais rendu ce dernière service.

Chère madame, ma lettre à un double but, je voulais d'abord que vous connaissiez mon existence, je vis avec mon mari et ma fille dont le mari est mobilisé.

Maintenant, comme je ne possède qu'une trés petite photographie de votre fils, voulez-vous bien, chère Madame, au nom de l'amitié qu'il m'as temoignie, m'en offrir une plus grande que je conserverai toujours.

En attendant je vous crie de croire a mes meilleurs sentiments affectueux et reconnaissants.

Mme Mialaret

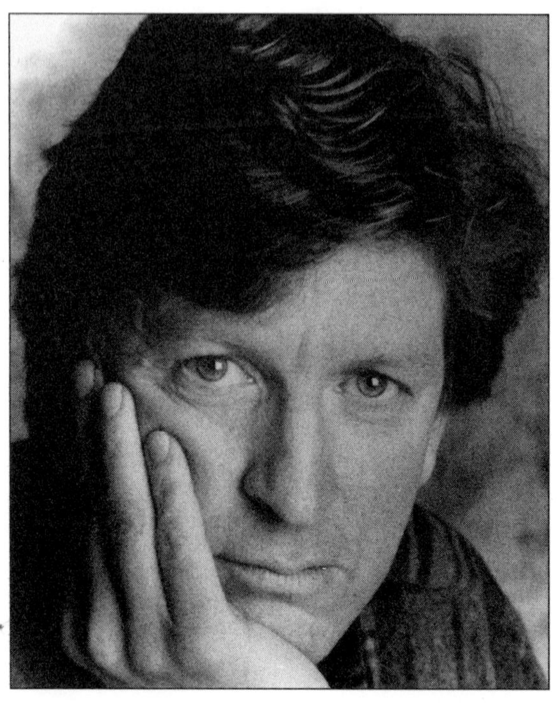

Actor/director R.H. Thomson has been working for more than 25 years in theatre, film and television. Winner of a Gemini, a Genie and a Dora Mavor Moore award in Canada, Thomson has achieved recognition through a series of diverse and memorable roles in all three mediums.

Born in Toronto, Thomson graduated from the University of Toronto with a Bachelor of Science and then went on to theatrical training at the National Theatre School in Montreal, and The London Academy of Music and Dramatic Art in England.

His interests have led him to host CBC's "Man Alive" series as well as advocating for cultural sovereignty and diversity on both national and international levels.